T0006000

DISNEP
RALPH
BREAKS THE
INTERNET

THE OFFICIAL GUIDE

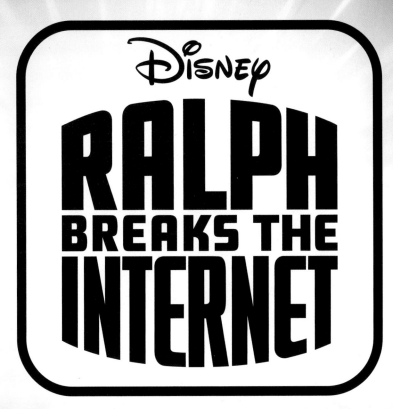

THE OFFICIAL GUIDE

Written by Matt Jones

CONTENTS ↓

Wreck-It Ralph

Vanellope
von Schweetz

INTRODUCTION

Wreck-It Ralph and Vanellope von Schweetz aren't your usual arcade-game heroes. These best friends are ready to take on a new mission to save Sugar Rush. They must venture to a new and exciting virtual world—the Internet!

WRECK-IT RALPH

Not-so-bad guy

Friendly and brave, Wreck-It Ralph was known only as the Bad Guy in the *Fix-It Felix, Jr.* arcade game, until he saved the whole arcade. While Ralph may still be the game's villain, he is now a hero and has a best friend in Vanellope, too.

Things you need to know about Ralph

1 Ralph thinks his life is perfect now in the arcade.

2 He really likes drinking root beer at the local tavern.

3 Ralph is very strong, but also very clumsy. He often accidentally breaks things!

4 Most of the arcade citizens used to avoid Ralph, but now they actually like him.

HAPPY HERO

For Ralph, life is perfect. He values his friendship with best pal Vanellope and loves to spend all of his free time with her. Ralph does not want his life to change!

Medal winner

Ralph has kept the hero's medal that Vanellope made for him. It is made out of a cookie and reads "To Stink Brain" on one side and "You're my hero" on the other.

VANELLOPE VON SCHWEETZ
Super racer

Daring and speedy, Vanellope is the best racer in the whole arcade! She loves racing and hanging out with her best friend, Ralph, but she wants an exciting new adventure, too.

Things you need to know about Vanellope

1 Vanellope is from a racing game named *Sugar Rush*.

2 She has the ability to glitch, which means she can teleport herself to another place.

3 Vanellope is the most popular character in *Sugar Rush*.

4 Ralph thinks Vanellope is the coolest kid around.

TOP RACER

Vanellope often wins the races in her *Sugar Rush* game and likes bragging about it. The only problem is that even though she loves her game, the current racetracks can be a bit boring.

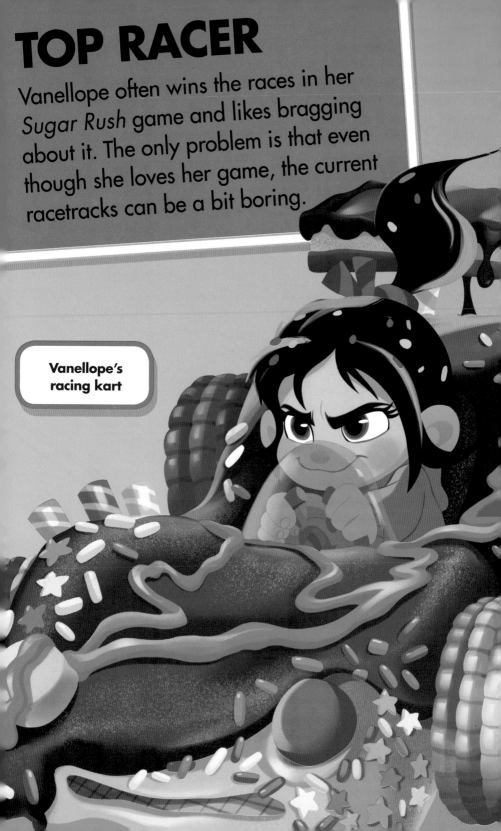

Vanellope's racing kart

Chocolate
fudge sauce

New track

Wanting to please Vanellope, Ralph
creates a new track, which branches
off from a normal one. It is full of twists,
turns, fallen candy cane trees, and
features a scary jump. Vanellope loves it!

TRUE OR FALSE?

Vanellope made
her racing kart
by herself.

False: Ralph and
Vanellope made her
racing kart together.

Cookie wheel

FIX-IT FELIX, JR.

Heroic handyman

Felix is the adored hero of his game, Fix-It Felix, Jr., and he's a great guy outside of it, too. It takes something really terrible to dampen his endlessly happy mood.

Things you need to know about Felix

1 Felix has a powerful golden hammer. He can fix any broken object by hitting it with the tool!

2 He is happily married to Sergeant Tamora Jean Calhoun, a strong fighter from *Hero's Duty*.

3 He is a great cook and does most of the cooking in the family.

4 While Felix's job is to beat Ralph in their game, the pair are good friends outside of it.

SERGEANT CALHOUN

Space warrior

Sergeant Calhoun is a brave, tough, and skilled fighter from *Hero's Duty*, a first-person shooter game. She endlessly fights to protect the galaxy from alien invaders.

Things you need to know about Calhoun

1 In Hero's Duty, Calhoun leads a squad of marines into battle every single day.

2 Calhoun lives with her husband in Niceland, the town in the *Fix-It Felix, Jr.* game.

3 Sergeant Calhoun is an expert hand-to-hand fighter and a skilled markswoman.

4 Her first name is Tamora, but most characters call her by her surname—Calhoun.

FELIX AND CALHOUN'S APARTMENT

Felix and Calhoun share a luxury apartment located in a tall building in Niceland. They both relax here after their busy days being heroes!

Furniture in perfect condition

🔍 Did you know?

Felix and Calhoun often host amazing parties for all their friends in the arcade.

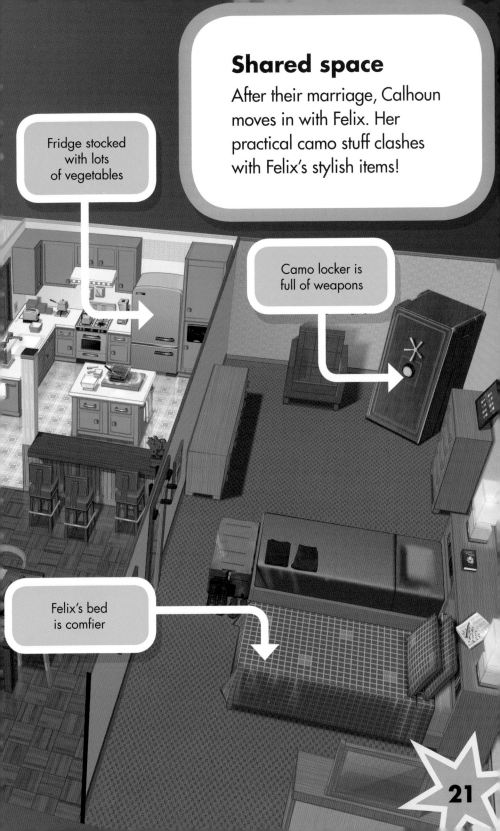

Shared space

After their marriage, Calhoun moves in with Felix. Her practical camo stuff clashes with Felix's stylish items!

Fridge stocked with lots of vegetables

Camo locker is full of weapons

Felix's bed is comfier

NEW PARENTS

When the plug is pulled on *Sugar Rush*, its residents are made homeless! Felix and Calhoun kindly offer to adopt the fifteen young racers, but they prove to be quite the handful! The couple must complete a range of tasks to care for these kids.

1 Cook a delicious healthy meal.

2 Fix anything broken by the racers around the apartment.

5 Stop the racers from completely destroying the apartment.

4 Try to stop the food fight!

3 Make sure the racers eat their vegetables.

LITWAK'S ARCADE

Litwak's Family Fun Center and Arcade is a great place to visit. From *Hero's Duty* to *Fix-it Felix, Jr.*, it is packed full of retro and modern arcade games to play.

Kids' outdoor play area

Shaded seating area

Q Did you know?

When the arcade closes, the arcade characters have lots of fun, spending time with each other or exploring other games.

Litwak's office

Stan Litwak's office is a small back room in the arcade. It is very messy and full of weird odds and ends.

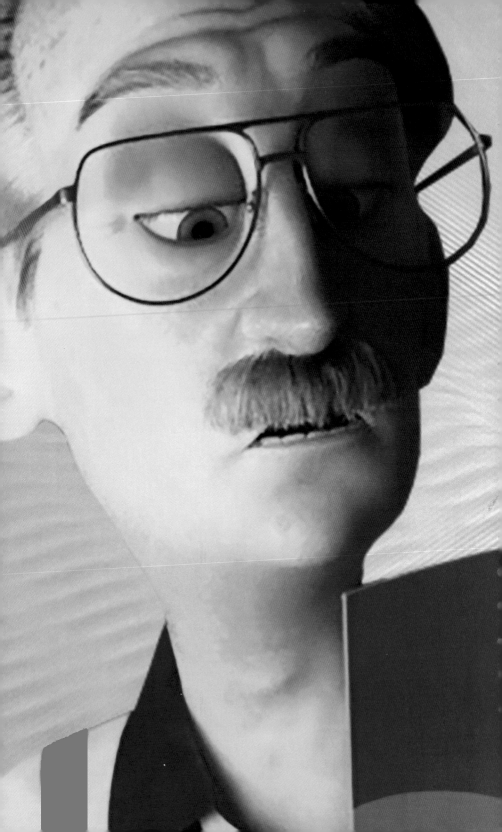

MR. LITWAK

Arcade owner

Friendly and fun, Stan Litwak is the owner of Litwak's Family Fun Center and Arcade. He has absolutely no idea that the games' characters are alive!

Things you need to know about Mr. Litwak

1 Litwak's Family Fun Center and Arcade has been open for more than 35 years.

2 Mr. Litwak knows lots about arcade machines, but hardly anything about Wi-Fi routers!

3 He does his best to keep games going, but sometimes he has to unplug them permanently.

Pulled plug

If a game breaks, there's a risk that it might be unplugged. The characters have to get to Game Central Station, or they will be lost forever!

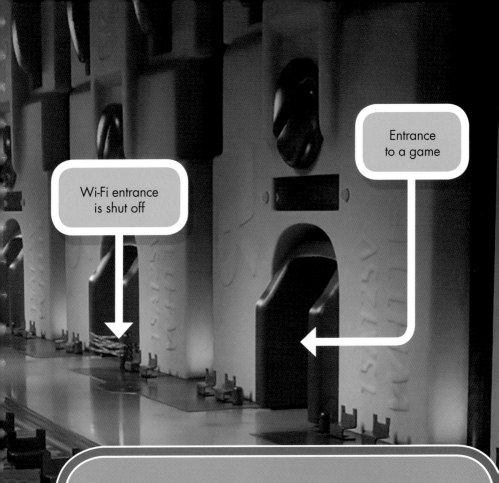

Wi-Fi entrance is shut off

Entrance to a game

GAME CENTRAL STATION

Game Central Station is a virtual space that looks like a train station and links all the arcade games. Characters can travel from one game to another, but they have to be back in their game when the arcade opens!

SUGAR RUSH

Plugged into the arcade in 1997, *Sugar Rush* is a racing car game based in a world full of sugary delights. It was ruled by the evil King Candy for decades, but six years ago was set free thanks to Ralph and Vanellope.

Old machine

The company that made *Sugar Rush* shut down years ago. Mr. Litwak can't easily buy new parts for it should anything break.

Candy lights up during game

Broken-down

While playing as Vanellope, a player accidentally breaks the game's steering wheel, and Litwak can't fix it. If Vanellope and Ralph can't find a new one for sale on the Internet, Litwak will get rid of the game!

Sugar Rush **steering wheel**

"Power Up" button activates a character's special ability

SURGE PROTECTOR

Law and order

Strict and bossy, Surge Protector has a very important role in the arcade. He works as a security guard in Game Central Station and keeps an eye out for any electrical faults.

Things you need to know about Surge Protector

1 He does his best to stop video game characters leaving their games when they shouldn't!

2 Surge appreciates a tip-off if there is a crime going on.

3 He is terrified of the *Sugar Rush* racers. He thinks they are basically feral!

CITIZENS OF LITWAK'S ARCADE

There are many different games in the arcade, and each one of them is full of weird and wonderful characters.

Taffyta Muttonfudge

Taffyta is one of the fifteen racers in *Sugar Rush*. She is mean to Vanellope because she is jealous of her skills.

Sour Bill

This grouchy sour ball named Bill is homeless after *Sugar Rush* shuts down, so he moves in with Gene.

Sparkly helmet is covered in sugar

Bill never looks happy

Cute bow

Candy

This red candy's favorite *Sugar Rush* racer is Swizzle Malarkey.

Plastic dress worn by many candies

Peanut Butter Cup

This candy loves to watch races. She is super upset when *Sugar Rush* is turned off.

Expensive cashmere cardigan

Gene

Gene is the wealthy mayor of Niceland, the fancy town in the game named *Fix-It Felix, Jr.*

WHICH IS YOUR FAVORITE ARCADE GAME?

Discover what arcade video game suits you the best! What would you play?

1 **What's your favorite activity?**

A Fighting aliens
B Racing
C DIY

2 **What's your preferred outfit?**

A Body armor
B Comfy clothes
C Handy coveralls

3 **How would you describe your personality?**

A Courageous
B Enthusiastic
C Optimistic

4 What would be your ideal hangout?

A Another planet
B A place with lots of candy
C A luxury apartment

5 What's your favorite way to get around?

A High-tech spaceship
B Racing kart
C Hopping

Mostly "A"s
Hero's Duty

Like Calhoun, you are a brave fighter willing to defend humanity.

Mostly "B"s
Sugar Rush

Like Vanellope, you are a keen racer who wants to win!

Mostly "C"s
Fix-it Felix, Jr.

Like Felix, you are a happy handyperson able to fix anything.

THE WI-FI

When Mr. Litwak plugs the Wi-Fi router into the arcade, it connects to Game Central Station. The Wi-Fi acts as a portal that allows the characters to travel to the Internet!

Litwak's avatar

Vanellope and Ralph are surprised to see a virtual version of Litwak, called an avatar, in the Wi-Fi router.

WI-FI CAPSULE

Wi-Fi capsules enclose the avatars traveling from Wi-Fi routers to the Internet. Vanellope enjoys the thrilling ride, but Ralph doesn't.

Vanellope holds on tight so she doesn't fall out of her seat

Holoscreens show key information

Ralph's trip

Unfortunately for Ralph, Wi-Fi capsules are designed for avatars, not him. His journey isn't very comfortable at all!

Vanellope's Wi-Fi capsule

Cable treks

The capsules move up the cables at really high speeds to the Internet.

Cute bunny websites pop up everywhere

Surfing the net

Ralph and Vanellope are in awe of the Internet. They are easily distracted from their mission to save *Sugar Rush*.

Cat websites litter the Internet

THE INTERNET

The Internet—or the net—is an amazing and crazy place, full of countless websites. Each page has a virtual building in the Internet. There are lots of great things to do and to see. But be careful, there are also terrible dangers, like viruses.

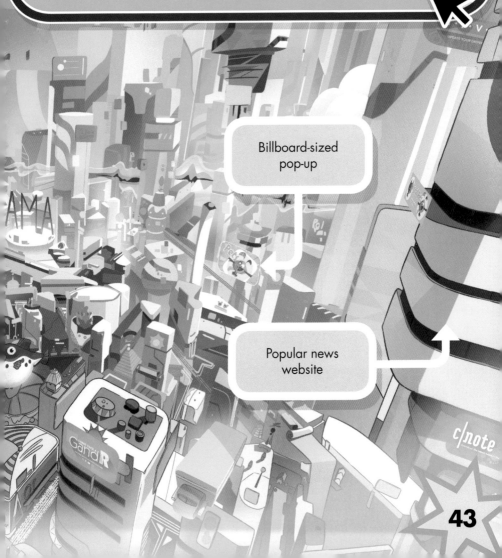

Billboard-sized pop-up

Popular news website

THE HUB

The Hub is a busy site on the Internet. It is the place where all the avatars arrive after they travel from their own Wi-Fi routers.

Avatars land on these spots

Around the globe

This hologram of the globe shows the locations that all of the avatars are arriving from.

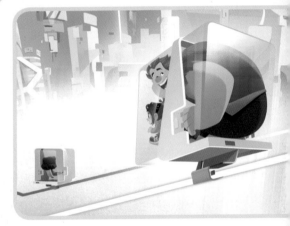

Fast track

Avatars and netizens can get quickly from website to website by hitching a ride in a vehicle called a pod. They aren't designed for tall Ralph, so it is sometimes a tight fit!

IN THE NET

Billions of different characters can be found in the Internet. There are two main types of characters: netizens and avatars.

Netizens

Netizens live and work in the net. From click baiters to pop-up blockers, there are many different jobs. Without the netizens, the net would not work at all!

Avatars' heads are all cuboid in shape

Avatars

Whenever a real person opens the Internet on a device, a copy of them, named an avatar, enters the virtual net. An avatar goes to each site that their counterpart wants to visit.

An avatar's style mimics that of their real life counterpart

Q KNOWSMORE
Smart helper

KnowsMore is a keen netizen. He works at a search bar, where avatars can ask him anything they want. He is very smart and knows more than anyone else!

Things you need to know about KnowsMore

1 KnowsMore is really quick-witted, and likes guessing what people are going to ask him.

2 He can find millions of search results incredibly quickly.

3 Unfortunately, some netizens are irritated by KnowsMore guessing what they want to ask!

4 KnowsMore is quite formal and dresses very smartly.

SEARCH

eBay

This awesome website is like a giant auction house with lots of auctions happening at the same time. From potato chips shaped like celebrities to paintings of kittens, there is an endless amount of stuff for avatars to bid on.

Ralph and Vanellope stand out among the avatars

Bidding frenzy

Ralph and Vanellope find the *Sugar Rush* steering wheel is up for auction. They don't understand how an auction works and think it is a game. They outbid each other, driving up the wheel's price to 27, 001 US dollars!

Each booth has a different item up for auction

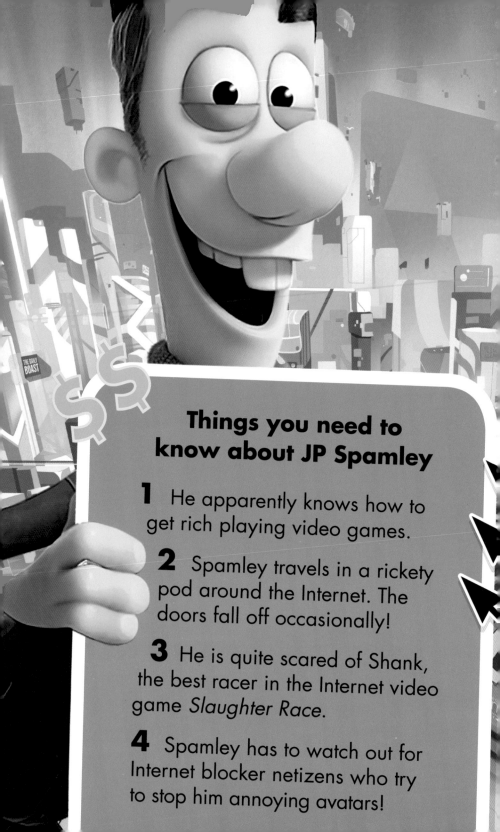

Things you need to know about JP Spamley

1 He apparently knows how to get rich playing video games.

2 Spamley travels in a rickety pod around the Internet. The doors fall off occasionally!

3 He is quite scared of Shank, the best racer in the Internet video game *Slaughter Race*.

4 Spamley has to watch out for Internet blocker netizens who try to stop him annoying avatars!

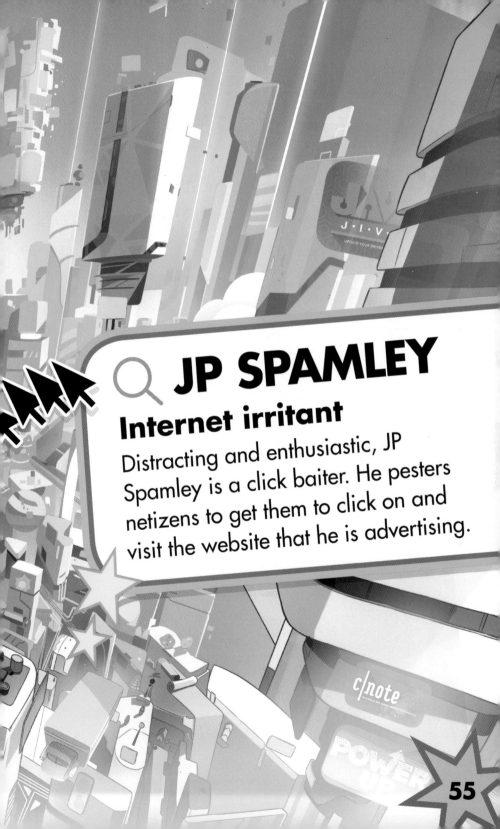

🔍 JP SPAMLEY

Internet irritant

Distracting and enthusiastic, JP Spamley is a click baiter. He pesters netizens to get them to click on and visit the website that he is advertising.

GORD

Spamley's assistant

This silent, sweater-wearing netizen is JP Spamley's right-hand man. Gord uses his really stretchy arms to quickly pass adverts to his boss.

Things you need to know about Gord

1 His full name is Gordon, but most netizens shorten his name and call him Gord.

2 Two of his cousins are Double Dan and Little Dan.

3 Gord has made a few viruses in his time, but he is not an expert.

4 His sweater is incredibly cozy and warm.

LOOTHUNTR.COM

Compared to BuzzzTube or eBay, JP Spamley's website, named Loothuntr.com, is far smaller and a little less high-tech. Any avatar that clicks on Spamley's link is transported to this disorganized office, which is slightly smelly and full of junk!

Gaming loot litters office

Potential loot kept on file

Helping hand

Spamley buys and sells items that Internet gamers need for their games. He tells Vanellope and Ralph to bring him Shank's car from *Slaughter Race*, and he can sell it for 40,000 US dollars.

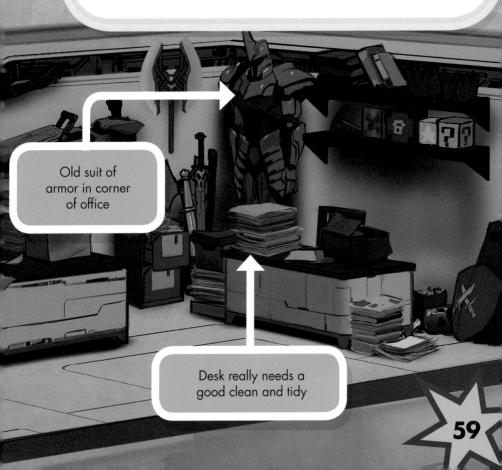

Old suit of armor in corner of office

Desk really needs a good clean and tidy

SLAUGHTER RACE

Slaughter Race is the fastest, most difficult racing game on the net. It is a Massively Multiplayer Online game, or MMO, which means lots of players can play it at once.

Ralph has never seen computer-generated smog

"Ok, this game is kind of amazing."

Vanellope

Sign says "*Slaughter Race*"

Danger zone

Slaughter Race is a dangerous world and threats lurk around every corner. There are lots of explosions, things to crash into, and massive sharks in the sewers!

Nasty netizens

Just like the rest of the Internet, netizens live in *Slaughter Race*. Most of them look terrifying and try to stop the players.

61

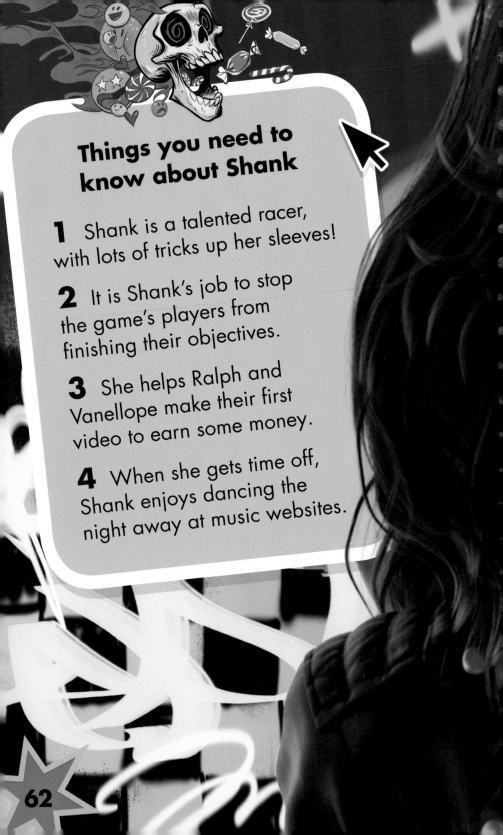

Things you need to know about Shank

1 Shank is a talented racer, with lots of tricks up her sleeves!

2 It is Shank's job to stop the game's players from finishing their objectives.

3 She helps Ralph and Vanellope make their first video to earn some money.

4 When she gets time off, Shank enjoys dancing the night away at music websites.

🔍 SHANK

Legendary racer

Shank is the boss of the *Slaughter Race* Internet racing game. She rules over this website with her gang.

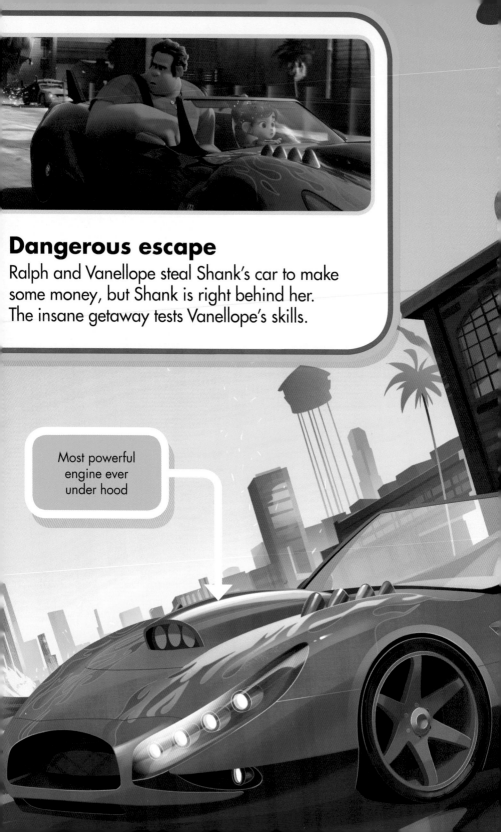

Dangerous escape

Ralph and Vanellope steal Shank's car to make
some money, but Shank is right behind her.
The insane getaway tests Vanellope's skills.

Most powerful
engine ever
under hood

SHANK'S CAR

Shank's car is the fastest, meanest, most powerful vehicle in the whole of *Slaughter Race*. Players are always trying to steal it, but they have to get past Shank first!

"That car is gorgeous."
Vanellope

Rear fins look super cool

Shank likes flames

SHANK'S GANG

This gang may look scary, especially if they are chasing you in *Slaughter Race*, but they are actually really nice. They work together to stop the players completing their missions. It's in their code!

Debbie

Like all the gang, Debbie sees the other members as her family. When she isn't racing, she often hangs out at a basketball court.

Flower tattoo from an in-game tattoo artist

66

Did you know?

Vanellope really enjoys hanging out with Shank and her crew. They are far friendlier than the *Sugar Rush* racers.

Pyro

Carrying two massive flamethrowers and a powerful leaf blower, Pyro will either burn a player's avatar or blow them away. Watch out!

67

Things you need to know about Yesss

1 Yesss is a smart, creative netizen who can figure out what is popular on the Internet.

2 She constantly changes her stunning look to match the latest new fashion trends.

3 Yesss only wants the most original content on her website.

4 She can be very hands on and edits videos to perfection.

🔍 YESS

Trend setter

Yesss is the head algorithm in charge at BuzzzTube, a video sharing website full of videos. She's always on the lookout for the next big thing to break the Internet!

Feline superstar

One of BuzzzTube's greatest stars is a grumpy-looking, chubby cat that likes squeezing into glass jars. This cat gets lots of hearts from avatars.

TRUE OR FALSE?

The Internet is full of cats and babies.

True: They are two of the most popular things!

Yesss proudly shows off BuzzzTube to Vanellope

BUZZZTUBE

BuzzzTube is the most popular video sharing site on the Internet. Avatars stop by the page to watch the videos and leave a heart if they like it. These hearts can be turned into money, and it can be a quick way to get rich!

Maybe

Maybe is the name of Yesss's long-serving, and long-suffering, assistant. He helps her keep track of what is trending and what isn't.

VIDEO MAKER

Ralph and Vanellope have to make some money fast, so they start creating videos. Will Ralph break the Internet?

1 Shank has a great idea for a video. She films Ralph's face being blown with a leaf blower.

3 Avatars love watching Ralph's video and leave lots of hearts. Ralph and Vanellope will make enough money in no time!

2 The video is put up on BuzzzTube. When an avatar likes it, they leave a heart. These hearts can be changed into lots of money!

OHMYDISNEY.COM

OhMyDisney.com is the best fan site on the entire Internet! Fans visit this enchanting website to meet some of their favorite characters.

"Wow, this place is bonkers!"

Vanellope

Classic Disney castle houses the website

OH MY DISNEY

Sparkling banner excites approaching avatars

A new friend

Vanellope quickly persuades the Princesses that she is
one of them. They offer Vanellope some great advice.

Drapes can be closed if
a Princess wants privacy

THE GREEN ROOM

After performing on stage to their adoring fans' avatars, the Princesses' avatars relax and unwind in their luxurious Green Room. Only Princesses are allowed in, so they are all quite surprised when Vanellope turns up!

Each Princess has their own cubbyhole

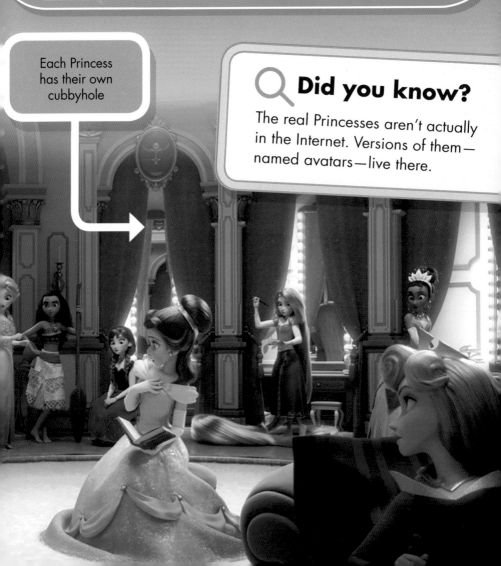

🔍 Did you know?

The real Princesses aren't actually in the Internet. Versions of them—named avatars—live there.

MEET THE COMFY SQUAD

Cinderella is inspired by Vanellope's comfy clothes. She asks her mice to make casualwear for all the Princesses.

Ariel

Ariel keeps a collection of treasured items in her cubbyhole.

Ariel can't believe she gets to wear a shirt

TRUE OR FALSE?

Is Vanellope actually a Princess?

True: Yes, Vanellope is a Princess in the video game Sugar Rush!

Tiana

Tiana is used to working all the time, but she's enjoying relaxing.

"NOLA" stands for New Orleans, Louisiana

Pocahontas

Pocahontas likes hanging out in her new outfit with Meeko.

Necklace given to her by her mother

Snow White has kept the poisonous apple

Snow White

Snow White is great at giving advice, and tells Vanellope to follow her destiny.

COMFY SQUAD CONTINUED

Anna often braids her hair in pigtails

Shirt reads "Just let it go"

Elsa

Elsa likes chilling out in between shows and fan quizzes.

Anna

Anna is surprised to hear that Vanellope is a Princess, since she does not look like one.

Belle

Belle keeps lots of books in her cubbyhole, so she always has one to hand.

Belle reads to relax

Mushu design on back of cool jacket

Hair kept free of accessories

Mulan

Mulan is always prepared to protect her friends with her sharp sword.

Rapunzel

Rapunzel keeps a frying pan in the Green Room just in case of intruders!

COMFY SQUAD CONTINUED

Jasmine

Jasmine lets her pet tiger, Rajah, into the Green Room, but the other Princesses aren't scared.

Jasmine's favorite chips

Cinderella

Cinderella absolutely loves Vanellope's comfy clothes.

Glass slippers replaced with comfier shoes

Aurora

Aurora is skilled at making rope. She can braid it really quickly.

Shirt reads "Nap Queen"

Hair always worn casual and messy

Heart of Te Fiti necklace

Moana

Moana enjoys drinking fresh, tasty coconut water.

Merida

Merida tells Vanellope to think about what she really wants in her life.

85

Things you need to know about Double Dan and Little Dan

1 They lurk in a lower level of the Internet, full of old websites.

2 Double Dan is one of the best virus makers in the Internet.

3 Little Dan helps his brother by uncorking bottles for him.

4 Double Dan puts some of his nastier viruses in wooden boxes.

🔍 DOUBLE DAN
And Little Dan

Double Dan is a worm-like netizen who makes viruses. Don't look at Little Dan, his brother who is growing out of his neck. It makes Double Dan really angry!

DOUBLE DAN'S LAB

Double Dan and Little Dan work in a filthy, cluttered lab in the Dark Net. The lab is packed full of horrible ingredients to make evil viruses.

Virus canister

Evil code

Malware

Storage shelves

WHICH INTERNET CHARACTER ARE YOU?

From cool Yesss to shifty Double Dan, there are many different netizens in the net. Which one are you most like?

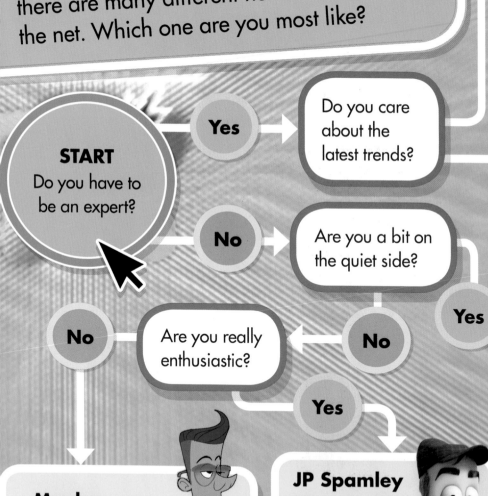

START
Do you have to be an expert?

Yes → Do you care about the latest trends?

No → Are you a bit on the quiet side?

Yes

Are you really enthusiastic? ← **No**

No

Yes

Maybe
Uncertain assistant, trend tracker

JP Spamley
Energetic click baiter, loot hunter

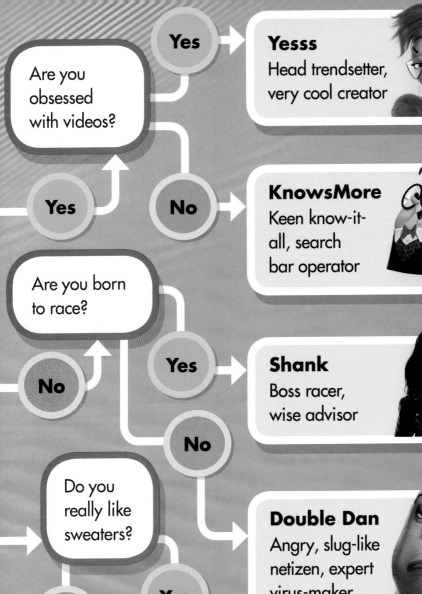

Are you obsessed with videos?

Yes →

Yesss
Head trendsetter, very cool creator

No →

KnowsMore
Keen know-it-all, search bar operator

Yes ↑

Are you born to race?

Yes →

Shank
Boss racer, wise advisor

No ↑

No

Do you really like sweaters?

No ↓

Yes

Double Dan
Angry, slug-like netizen, expert virus-maker

Little Dan
Silent partner, hanger-on

Gord
Cozy sweater-wearer, handy helper

🔍 GLOSSARY

Auction
An event where someone sells an item by letting others offer an amount of money for it. The person who offers the most money wins and has to pay for it.

Avatar
A virtual version of a real-life person who visits the Internet.

BuzzzTube
A trendy website where avatars can go and watch videos.

Code
A set of instructions that makes every virtual character and place who or what they are.

eBay
A website where you can buy or sell items via an auction.

Green Room
A room where performers can relax before or after a show.

The Hub

The first page an avatar visits in the Internet.

Netizen

A virtual person that lives and works in the Internet.

Pod

A vehicle used to travel between sites in the Internet.

Virus

An evil bit of code that can disrupt websites.

Wi-Fi capsule

A see-through vehicle that transports avatars from the Wi-Fi router to the Internet.

Wi-Fi router

A machine that connects a computer to the Internet.

"You will always be my best friend. Always."

Vanellope to Ralph

Written and edited by Matt Jones
Designers Chris Gould and Jess Tapolcai
Pre-production Producer Kavita Varma
Senior Producer Mary Slater
Managing Editor Sadie Smith
Managing Art Editor Vicky Short
Publisher Julie Ferris
Art Director Lisa Lanzarini
Publishing Director Simon Beecroft

First American Edition, 2018
Published in the United States by DK Publishing
345 Hudson Street, New York, New York 10014

Page design copyright © 2018 Dorling Kindersley Limited
DK, a Division of Penguin Random House LLC

18 19 20 21 22 10 9 8 7 6 5 4 3 2 1

002–307136–Oct/2018

Published in Great Britain by Dorling Kindersley Limited.

A catalog record for this book is available from the Library of Congress.

ISBN: 978-1-4654-6660-0

DK books are available at special discounts when purchased in bulk for sales promotions, premiums, fund-raising, or educational use. For details, contact: DK Publishing Special Markets, 345 Hudson Street, New York, New York 10014 SpecialSales@dk.com

Printed and bound in the USA

A WORLD OF IDEAS:
SEE ALL THERE IS TO KNOW

www.dk.com
www.disney.com